IMAGES
of America

NASHUA
IN TIME AND PLACE

The Hunt Memorial Building, once the Nashua Public Library, is now the cultural center of the community. Chimes from the clock tower signal the passing time of day. Pictured is the Hunt Memorial Building at night with its illuminated clock tower and Gothic windows. The Hunt building is currently being restored to its original splendor by the Hunt Memorial Building Committee. (Courtesy of Nashua Public Library.)

(Cover photograph: Courtesy of Alan Sewell.)

IMAGES
of America

NASHUA
IN TIME AND PLACE

Trustees of the Hunt Building

ARCADIA
PUBLISHING

Published by Arcadia Publishing
Charleston, South Carolina

Library of Congress Catalog Card Number: 9961278

For all general information contact Arcadia Publishing at:
Telephone 843-853-2070
Fax 843-853-0044
E-mail sales@arcadiapublishing.com
For customer service and orders:
Toll-Free 1-888-313-2665

Visit us on the Internet at www.arcadiapublishing.com

Dedication

This picture book is for you.
May it rekindle the flame
of memories past.

Meri Goyette, 1999

CONTENTS

INTRODUCTION

Nashua: In Time and Place is a kaleidoscopic and nostalgic journey of photography in Nashua from its earliest years through the 1970s. Nashua, New Hampshire, is an extraordinary city. Twice in ten years Nashua was selected by *Money Magazine* as the number one city in all of America in which to live and work, a quintessential achievement for this unique city. This photographic history is at once a tribute and celebration to the memories of Mary A. and Mary E. Hunt, benefactors of the Hunt Memorial Library building, and to those citizens who, in the spirit and tradition of the Hunt family, have continued to contribute generously to the restoration of this historic, Renaissance building.

In the beginning, the township was called Dunstable. In 1837, its name became Nashua in recognition of the Nashua River. Waterway transportation was the engine that fueled the commercial and industrial growth of Nashua and its environs. The Merrimack River, with its locks in place, transported capital goods from Concord, Manchester, Nashua, and Lowell through the Middlesex Canal (completed in 1803) to Charlestown's Mill in Boston and beyond.

By this time, the village had become a city. The horse cars, sleds, and stagecoaches, along with steamboat forms of travel, were replaced by electric trolleys and a railroad system.

The surge of businesses and industrial activity between 1840–1900 accompanied an influx of Irish and French-Canadian immigrants. In turn, they were followed by a new wave of immigrant Poles, Greeks, Lithuanians, and Jews. This migration put the final social stamp on the city as we know it today. In recent years, Afro-Americans, Hispanics, and Asians were added to the city's population.

The Nashua Manufacturing Company, the Jackson Mills, White Mountain Freezer Company, Nashua Card and Glazed Paper Company, Estabrook and Anderson, Nashua Gas and Light Company, and a wide diversity of manufacturing companies were rapidly changing the village into a major industrial center. Downtown Nashua's Main Street and its environs were a beehive of activity, a place for the community to meet friends and neighbors and to shop. Woolworth, W.T. Grant Company, Phillip Morris, Speare Dry Goods, Atlantic and Pacific Tea Company, the Nashua Theatre, and a score of restaurants, candy stores, and tea-shops were firmly established. Greek, Lithuanian, Polish, and French-Canadian groceries, meat markets, and bakeries recalled delicious aromas of the Old World.

In 1948, after 125 years of continuous service, the textile mills left the city of Nashua. At first the city was devastated but quickly rebounded by explosive and unprecedented growth. Sanders Associates, an electronic and defense firm, was the first to come to Nashua and occupied the

Jackson Mills on Canal Street. The latter was followed by other research, high technology, computer, and software companies. The growth and prosperity of the city continued through the 1960s and beyond. New businesses and plants were established, which created new jobs, paid higher wages, and manufactured new products. In turn, new apartment complexes and neighborhoods of massive residential developments sprang up. New shopping plazas and malls were also constructed.

The population growth and the influx of engineers, researchers, electronic technicians, administrators, and managers spurred the proliferation of professional and cultural institutions within the city. New medical, legal, and banking offices opened, while older ones expanded and hospitals modernized. The Nashua Symphony Orchestra was resurrected, and the Nashua Choral Society, Arts and Science Center, Nashua Theater Guild, and the Actorsingers were founded. A new public library was built. Several new schools were built and a new Nashua Historical Society building was constructed.

Nashua: In Time and Place is more than a picture book—it preserves for history and generations to come the changing character of this Renaissance city.

—Joseph G. Sakey 1998

Acknowledgments

Nashua: In Time and Place had its beginning in a citywide photographic search project sponsored by the Hunt Memorial Building Trustees in the spring of 1998. The search produced more than 1,500 photographs from individual and institutional collections. Two hundred twenty photographs were chosen for this publication.

This book would not have been conceived or published without the cooperative efforts of many people, including a dedicated Board of Trustees: chair, Meri Goyette; honorable chair, Mayor Donald C. Davidson. Trustees Nancy Blish, Betty Gimber, Don Marquis, Frank Mellen, Sarah Roche, and Linda Willett gave unstinting encouragement and support.

Members of the Hunt Heritage Book Committee made significant contributions in time and talent for the preparation of the manuscript: Cynthia Kyriax Burney, Alice Gabriel, Frank Mellen, Frank Mooney, Patricia Ledoux, Donald Pickering, and Joseph G. Sakey. Advisers to the committee—Leonard Guerette, Jeannine Levesque, Michael Shalhoup, and Marilyn Solomon—generously shared their personal and professional knowledge of the history of Nashua.

A special thanks goes to Alan S. Manoian, Nashua Downtown Development specialist, for numerous Chapter One photographic and heritage interpretations.

The trustees are also grateful to Mayor Donald C. Davidson and the Board of Aldermen for their support of this project. Although no city funds were used in this publication, their continued encouragement of the restoration of the Hunt Memorial Building was vital.

Meri Goyette, chairperson of the Hunt Memorial Building Board of Trustees, spearheaded the overall direction of the project. Without her steadfastness and perseverance, the project would not have taken place.

The Board of Trustees is indebted and grateful to the following people and institutions, who made a major effort in sharing information and lending these photographs to the Hunt Heritage Book Committee: Dexter Arnold, Marie Barisano, Claire Phaneuf Boucher, Boys' Club of Nashua, Bronzecraft, Shirley Buder, Bullseye Color Photo, Inc., Peggy Caron, Vito and Mary Caprio, Roland Caron, Maurice Chagnon, M.D., Charles Colletta, Greg Coronis, David Cote, Lucille Cloutier, Mary Coutoumas, Louise Desclos, Eleanor Dorr, Joseph Drohan, Rita Duclos, Priscilla Flagg, Muriel Francoeur, Alice Gabriel, Lee Guerette Gidge, Lester Gidge, Betty Gove, Charles Goyette, M.D., Charles Grigas, Leonard Guerette, Richard Hall, Humane Society of N.E., Annabelle S. Johnson, Martha Johnson, Mr. and Mrs. Raymond E. Johnson, George Labrie, George Law, Jack Law, Patricia Ledoux, Evelyn Lyons, Si Mahfuz, Bernice Markewich, Roland

Maynard, Maynard and Lesieur, Jane and Don McAlman Sr., Richard and Elaine McAlpine, Leonard A. Rolfe, McDonald's Kitchenware Store, Marvis and Frank Mellen, Lennie Migneault, Mariette I. Moher, Frank Mooney, Nashua Public Library, Nashua Cemetery Association, John Nolan, Steve Norris, Katherine C. O'Neill, Bernard Pastor, Darlene Pelletier, Don Pickering, Proctor Animal Cemetery, Peter Prew, Rita Raucykevich, Mr. and Mrs. Ravenelle, Mr. and Mrs. Hyman Romer, Lucille Roy, St. Joseph Hospital, Sanders, a Lockheed Martin Company, Philip Scontsas, Joan Scontsas, Mike Shalhoup, Kristin J. Schofield, Alan Sewell, Muriel Shaw, Jafar Shoja, Virginia Smith, Barbara Tamposi, Gertrude Thibault, George Tsiaras, H. Robert Weisman, Gary Wingate, S. Robert Winer, WSMN, and YMCA. We extend our apologies for any omission to the credits given.

A special thanks goes to Florence Shepard, author of *the Nashua experience* and *Nashua New Hampshire: a pictorial history*. These books were used for research. The *Nashua Centennial* was also used as a source of reference.

—Hunt Building Board of Trustees

Note: Many people wanted to share their memories. Their pictures are representative; however, space requirements limited selections. For detailed and historical references to the area, the editor suggests *The Nashua Experience*, Florence Shepard editor; and *Nashua: A Pictorial History*, F. Shepard and Brian Lawrence.

One

PERSPECTIVES

"Dare to live while life is passing;
Set your heart upon a star.
Dance the moments into hours;
Sing the hours into years.

Time is all that life can give us—
Wanting more is having less;"

The Greeley Farm, given to the city in 1881 by Joseph Thornton Greeley, became a city park 30 years later. Greeley Park, located in the north end of Nashua on Concord Street is "a place to rest and enjoy nature." A gift of $5,000 by John E. Cotton, matched by city funds, allowed Greeley Farm to be converted into a public park in 1908. With gifts of additional land and landscaping, the area was improved. A stone and cement rest house, a fountain, a shallow pond, a gravel walk, and flower beds required the services of a caretaker during the summers.

This *c.* 1860 photograph shows travelers awaiting the train on a sunny morning at Nashua's Main Street Station. In 1838, the Nashua & Lowell Railroad, New Hampshire's first, began operations and linked with the (1835) Boston and Lowell Railroad. With the building of Nashua's first railroad station in 1848, Union Square, at the north side of the bridge, became Railroad Square. The station's upper level boasted the famed Franklin Opera House. Pictured is a wood-beam and stone abutment, Main Street Bridge, the Indian Head Coffee House (1803) atop the hill, and the Greeley Block (1833) below. The station and opera house were lost to fire in 1931.

This *c.* 1895 photograph looks south from the bridge to Main Street, the commercial and architectural heart of Nashua, as it rolls up the hill from the river's edge to Factory and Temple Streets. In 1886, the street railway company first placed tracks across the Main Street Bridge. Most noticeable on the left side are the First Congregational Church (1872), Nashua's first city hall (1843), and the Odd Fellows Building (1892). The Odd Fellows Building is the sole surviving architectural treasure, all others being destroyed by either fire or demolition to accommodate the twentieth-century widening of Main Street at the bridge.

The Tremont House (1848) and the Merchants Exchange Block (1876) are highly ornamented with patriotic bunting in celebration of Nashua's 1903 semi-centennial festivities. The Tremont, first known as the Pearl Street House, served the lodging and dining needs of the growing industrial city. The Tremont House location became known as Tremont Square. Visiting U.S. presidents and dignitaries gave orations from the hotel's grand balcony, erected in 1874. Franklin D. Roosevelt frequented the Tremont with his Groton School classmates, which he reminisced as "swanking around the Tremont." The historic Tremont Hotel was demolished in 1922 to accommodate the new Second National Bank building, erected in 1924.

The old steamer bellowing smoke was driven by Charles Farnsworth. This is a far cry from our modern-day fire equipment. The fire department was established in the early 1830s to promote fire protection. Originally private companies bought the first fire equipment. Later there were three engine companies, one hose company, and one hook and ladder company manned by about 150 men.

At the turn of the century, a trolley stop was located at Franklin and Main Streets in front of the Whiting Block and the Indian Head Bank. In 1902 a network of electric railways extended to Salem, as well as Canobie Lake Park and Haverhill, Massachusetts. Shortly thereafter this system was expanded to Concord and Boston. The dominance of this mode of transportation was cut short by the arrival of the automobile.

Constructed c. 1872, the First Congregational Church and the Phillips Block stand side by side as solid neighbors on Main Street. The 1870 fire that destroyed the original 1835 First Church also consumed the original structure standing on the site of the Phillips Block. The First Church and the Phillips Block were rebuilt together on the corner of Park and Main Streets by 1872. The Phillips Block housed Nashua's first modern post office. The Sargent Building, Nashua's first brick store and dwelling house, stands on the other side of the church. Both 1872 structures were lost to fire in the 1960s. The historic Sargent Building is also just a memory.

It was a quiet day at the Amherst Street fire station when its horse-drawn apparatuses were displayed. The fire department was of vital importance for the safety of the city. At first, one horse pulled the hose carriage. For expediency the horse would be harnessed by an overhead arrangement when a call was received. Much later, in 1922, Mayor Burque augmented the equipment of the fire department with the purchase of a new aerial ladder.

Located in 1870 at the top of Temple Street at the corner of Court and Church Streets, the Central Fire House was Nashua's first modern fire station. From the tower of the Central Station, one could survey a good part of the growing city. The Central Station was one of Nashua's proudest, post-Civil War achievements and marked the beginning of a great industrial, commercial, housing, capital, and labor expansion. The corner of the 1882 Pilgrim Church is visible at the right.

This rare, c. 1920 photograph, taken from the bell tower of Nashua's first town hall, built c. 1843, shows a view of Main Street looking north toward Library Hill and the finely located 1903 Hunt Memorial Library Building. This was the "Gateway to New Hampshire." Once over the bridge, across the river, and up the hill, travelers could choose to travel north to Manchester, Concord, and up to the White Mountains, or west to Amherst, the Monadnock Region, and on to Vermont. In the center is the Main Street Bridge, and off to the left is Water Street. The historic structures on the west side of Main Street were demolished after 1946 to widen Main Street and the bridge.

The trolleys ran this last day on Main Street in 1931. In front of the Indian Head Bank one can see the new mode of transportation, the motor-driven bus. At one time the route between Nashua and Lowell was the longest in the country. The first electric car service between the two cities started in 1895.

The old police station located on Court Street was built in 1890. In addition to being a police station, it housed the police court, jail, padded cell for violent prisoners, "tramp-room," and city morgue. It later became the home of the American Legion. As this photograph shows, the building was covered with ivy.

The 1903 Nashua Semi-Centennial Celebration official program states, "The City Hall was the center of the throng. . . Many times in the past Nashua has put on a festive appearance, but never had the city looked as well." The "Town Hall" was completed in the spring of 1843. The structure was 66 by 90 feet, and the height from the ground to the top of the cupola was about 100 feet. The town hall was located on the second floor and boasted moveable seating for 1,300 and a full gallery. The attic was finished for the use of drilling and marching military companies. Nashua's 1843 town hall was demolished in 1936.

This heartfelt patriotic demonstration followed the Fourth of July parade in 1918. On April 6, 1917, President Wilson had proclaimed a state of war with Germany. All men between 21 and 35 years of age were required to register for the draft. On November 11, 1918, World War I ended. Armistice terms were signed by Germany, and Nashua cheered the end of the war. At this time there was an abundance of grocery stores, dressmakers, music teachers, milliners, saloons, restaurants, and gathering places in town. Ankle-length skirts were in fashion for the

ladies, and gentlemen wore straw hats and spats. As seen in this photograph, Main Street was filled with bicycles, horse-drawn carriages, automobiles, and even a convertible touring car. Pedestrians were on the sidewalk and others attempted to cross the street. Onlookers peered from behind curtains in the block. The following year women's suffrage reform was put into effect giving women their right to vote.

17

Following the demolition of the 1843 Nashua City Hall, a new city hall and police station was designed by 1938 and completed and dedicated in 1939. The chosen site for the 1939 city hall was at the southern limit of what was then considered the core commercial district. Significant Victorian homes and the South Common dominated this area. However, the site abutted the busy Nashua-Worcester Railroad line, which ran along West Hollis Street. The architectural vernacular of the new city hall was significantly inspired by the 1843 town house and included the cupola of the original town hall.

This c. 1950 automobile traffic is headed south down Library Hill toward the Main Street Bridge. As the "Gate City," Nashua's heavily traveled Main Street profoundly influenced the city's heritage and identity. Main Street Nashua has served New Hampshire as the primary entry and departure point of the Merrimack River Valley. The tall central structure is the Dunlap Building, built c. 1865 by Archibald Dunlap, whose statesmanship resolved the disagreement over the location of the Civil War Soldiers and Sailors Monument (top right) in 1889. The Dunlap Building housed the Dunlap Seed Company and is located across Main Street from the Hunt Memorial Building.

18

The First Congregational Church is seen in the left foreground. In the background is the Tavern Hotel, the Hunt Memorial Building, and Whiting Block. The First Congregational Church was built in 1894. The Tavern Hotel, originally the Greeley Building, constructed in 1833, housed a produce store and was located where the Hunt Memorial Building now stands. It was moved in 1903 to Clinton Street to accommodate the Hunt Library.

In 1892, $50,000 was given to the City by Mary A. and Mary E. Hunt, wife and daughter of John M. Hunt, to erect a library building in his memory. This is a view of its main reading room. Because of the need for a more modern library, Eliot Carter, Nashua philanthropist, and his wife, Edith, gave Nashua the gift of a new library in 1968. The public library continues today as a modern facility on Court Street.

19

This modest building, known as the Pearl Street Schoolhouse (built c. 1893), was the site of an extraordinary social and educational experiment. The first kindergarten classroom opened on the corner of East Pearl and Quincy Streets. Jennie Farley, who taught first grade in Mount Pleasant in 1892, was Nashua's first kindergarten teacher. The superintendent of schools reported in 1895, "The enthusiasm with which this school has been received by both parents and children has raised it immediately from the position of an experiment to that of an established necessity."

The Arlington Street School, dedicated in 1890, served the increasingly populated Crown Hill neighborhood. It offered the most modern learning facilities in Nashua. The superintendent of schools stated in 1889, "The frequent languor and torpor of many rooms are directly attributable to vitiated air, either the means of ventilating being inadequate, or the teachers careless or both." He also added, "In the good time coming I trust that all our buildings will have the fresh air and genial warmth of the Arlington Street building." This progressive school building was later demolished.

In 1874, the Spring Street Cemetery lot was purchased, and in April 1875, a new, grand Nashua High School building was dedicated. It contained ten classrooms, a recitation room, two lecture rooms, a library room, a laboratory, offices for the principal and superintendent, and a third-floor assembly hall. In 1905, a new high school building was dedicated on Temple Street. On March 21, 1917, the Spring Street High School was destroyed by fire. In 1919 a new high school was dedicated on the site of the 1875 structure, with the Temple Street School then serving as the junior high school. The 1919 Spring Street High School was demolished in the late 1980s to make way for the new Hillsborough County Court House.

This photograph is of the Spring Street School after it was rebuilt in 1919. It served as a junior high school until it was demolished in the late 1980s to make room for the Hillsborough County Court House.

The old South Burial Ground and schoolhouse on the Lowell Road was described by Anabelle Spence as a place ". . . where, after funerals, I played when I was young. We took a flower from each memorial basket and put one on each grave if the person was under ten years of age." The cemetery was the first burial ground in Nashua and was established in the 1600s. Both the building and the burial ground remain today.

At the Proctor Cemetery for animals off Ferry Road, our 4-footed friends and other pets find their final rest. Established in the 1920s, it is now filled to capacity. M. Jennie Kendall was the founder of the cemetery. An epitaph reads as follows: "Summer breeze, blow gently, Summer sun shine bright, Lightly lie the sod above you, Good night, 'Pal' good night." Jennie Kendall also had the distinction of being the first woman ever named deputy sheriff in the state.

In November 1847, the Third Orthodox Congregational Society dedicated their new church, known as the Third Congregational Church, or the Pearl Street Church, at the corner of East Pearl and Main Streets. Dunstable's first Universalist Society formed in January 1818. They erected their church building c. 1839 on the west side of Main Street near High Street. In 1881, the Universalists purchased the Pearl Street Church. In 1953, the historic structure was sold to the Nashua Trust Company. Though no longer a church, the building has survived.

Dedicated on June 27, 1827, the Unitarian Church on Lowell Street is Nashua's oldest standing church building. The architect of the Greek Revival structure is believed to be Asher Benjamin, the first agent of the 1823 planned manufacturing town. Concerning the dedication the church history states, "The church will open at half-past ten. . . . The council (of men) will assemble at the house of Daniel Abbot, Esq. and at eleven will move in procession to the church." Daniel Abbot was founder of the Nashua Manufacturing Company and the Nashua & Lowell Railroad.

The fire on Crown Hill on May 4, 1930, was one of the most disastrous events in the city's history. The blaze began on a windy day on a footbridge near a Boston & Maine trestle and spread to the end of town, causing a million-dollar loss of homes and businesses. It left 350 families homeless; a quarter of the city was destroyed. Fire departments from as far away as Boston came to assist.

The fire left much of that section of Nashua a barren land, destroying many homes and businesses. Starting on a Sunday afternoon, the fire spread rapidly from Canal Street, across Temple Street, down Spruce Street, and across East Hollis Street. Crown Hill became a mass of destruction.

This 1951 photograph shows Nashua firemen fighting flames in this building, Philips Block, on the corner of Park and Main Streets. Phillips Block had been built in 1872. It is now the site of the Allen Building. Lost in this fire was the Bargain Outlet as well as Nashua Hardware and Plumbing.

The Merchants Exchange Building at Main and High Streets looked like an "Ice Palace" after this fire in February of 1930, which nearly destroyed the north end of the building. This well-constructed block had been built in 1870 replacing Gaskin's Paint Shop and the Fuller Harness shop. This structure still stands, housing Martha's Exchange and other businesses. It is a prime example of mercantile buildings of the era. It was in this building that "Mitch" Fokas served Nashuans from behind the counter at Martha's Sweet Shoppe.

Canal Street looks east in this scene with the bell steeple of St. Francis Xavier Church in view during the great flood of 1936. Heavy winter snow melted during mid-March, and the rains that followed had much of Nashua underwater for several days.

Due to the flood of 1936, the train schedule was obviously interrupted at Nashua Union Station. The Union Station was built in 1860 and remained in operation until 1965, when it was demolished. The railroad served as a vital link to the north to Concord and beyond and to the south to Lowell and Boston, keeping goods and services moving.

Another natural disaster visited Nashua. The crushing power of the Hurricane Carol of 1954 is evident in this view of the Nashua Manufacturing parking lot. Nashuans again struggled with a clean-up of the area. Trees were toppled and caused an estimated half-million dollars worth of damage. However, strong community spirit prevailed and it was not long until things were back to normal. (Courtesy of *The Telegraph*, photographed by Mike Shalhoup.)

On November 12, 1954, the *Red Wing Express*, the Montreal to Boston train, loaded with commuters, was wrecked at Bridge Street Crossing. One person was killed and 21 were injured. The train wreck was the number-one story in New England covered by the Associated Press. Nashua resident Mike Shalhoup worked at *The Telegraph* for nearly four decades as a photographer, reporter, and editor. The building in upper left center is the Nashua Farmers Exchange. (Courtesy of *The Telegraph*, photographed by Mike Shalhoup.)

The Nashua Boat Club was incorporated in 1895, and the boathouse was dedicated in July 1896. The mission of the club stated, "The encouragement of boating and the athletic sports, to promote physical culture, and foster a unity of feeling among those interested in rowing and canoeing in Nashua." It was reported soon after that "The club was met with the most flattering reception by the citizens . . ." It included tennis and croquet courts, as well as private boat and canoe docks to accommodate a flotilla. The turn-of-the-century boathouse is long gone.

The Fish Hatchery on Broad Street across from the Nashua Mall is "dedicated to the wise use of our fish and wildlife resources." Many national fish hatcheries in the Northeast regions raise one or more species of trout or salmon. In 1865, Mayor Virgil C. Gilman, Dr. Edward Spaulding, and others built the first fish hatchery known in southern New Hampshire. From this project came the present hatchery, which is now owned and controlled by the federal government since 1898 and is part of the Federal Atlantic Reclamation Project.

President William Howard Taft laid the cornerstone of the YMCA's first home on Temple Street and the corner of Spring Street on March 19, 1912. The Nashua YMCA was established on October 6, 1877, with rooms at 69 Main Street. The original purpose of the organization was for religious training and social work for boys.

A banner marked the celebration of the golden anniversary of the YMCA at the corner of Temple and Spring Street. The first meeting to consider the funding of the YMCA was held in 1887. The property was bought through a legacy of Mary B. and Charles H. Nutt. In 1912, a gymnasium was built on the adjoining lot on Temple Street, and a cornerstone was laid by President William H. Taft.

"Meet you at the Rosebud" was the message. During the 1940s and '50s, friends would meet at the Rosebud at the corner of Main and West Hollis Streets for a snack and make plans to see the famous Duke Ellington and his orchestra at the Tremont Theater or take in a movie featuring Don Ameche and Andrea Leeds at the State Theater.

Maynard and Lesieur was one of the first area businesses to service the growing members of the auto-driving public. As the popularity of automotive transportation increased, the other forms of transportation decreased. Having been located in the downtown for 70 years, Roland M. Lesieur is still actively involved in the business and specializes in automotive tires. The steeple in the rear was part of the Londonderry Spring Water Company, which burned down in the 1980s.

In 1823, the Nashua Manufacturing Company was incorporated. The introduction of large-scale manufacturing, which created a "laboring class," profoundly transformed agrarian and mercantile Dunstable into the industrial and urban Nashua. A manufacturing community lives and works by the clock of the factory. The mill bell and clock tower dominated the daily activities of Nashua's laboring population. Mill No. 2, pictured above, was in operation by 1828. The clock tower, erected *c.* 1860, originally held a bell. In 1880, the now familiar clock, built by Howard & Company, was introduced into the tower at a cost of $525.

A "birds-eye view" shows Laton Hotel, Deschenes Oval, Hammar Hardware, Tavern Hotel, Maffee's Garage, and the First Congregational Church. The Laton House welcomed its first patrons in July of 1881. "Rooms at $2.00 and a menu of repasts for $1.00." Guests from all over New England considered the Laton Hotel to be the finest facility of its time. This historic section of Nashua is today being developed as an integral part of the downtown.

Nashua's City Poor Farm was established around 1853 to care for paupers, and after 1858, it also served as the House of Correction for up to 50 prisoners serving short terms for minor offenses. Adjacent to this building was the Pest House on Taylor Road for those with infectious diseases. The poor farm remained operational until July of 1908. Today it is the Nashua Country Club.

The modern facilities at the Nashua Country Club provide for activities including swimming, curling, tennis, and an 18-hole championship golf course. Providing a place for meetings and social events, it serves as an important part of the community.

The only route over the Nashua River in Hollis was by crossing the covered Runnell's Bridge on West Hollis Street. Another bridge in Nashua was the first Taylor Falls Bridge, built in 1827 by private investors, across the Merrimack River. This was a wooden, covered structure connecting Dunstable and Nottingham West (Hudson). Tolls were charged according to type of traffic. In 1854, it became a public right of way owned jointly by the two towns.

Phillips Block was the home of an early post office location at the corner of Park and Main Streets in 1883. The first post office was established in 1803 in a tavern in south Nashua. Mail arrived by stagecoach or post riders. In 1811, the post office was moved to the "Harbor," the home of Israel Hunt. His son, John M. Hunt, succeeded him and moved the office to the Hunt's General Store.

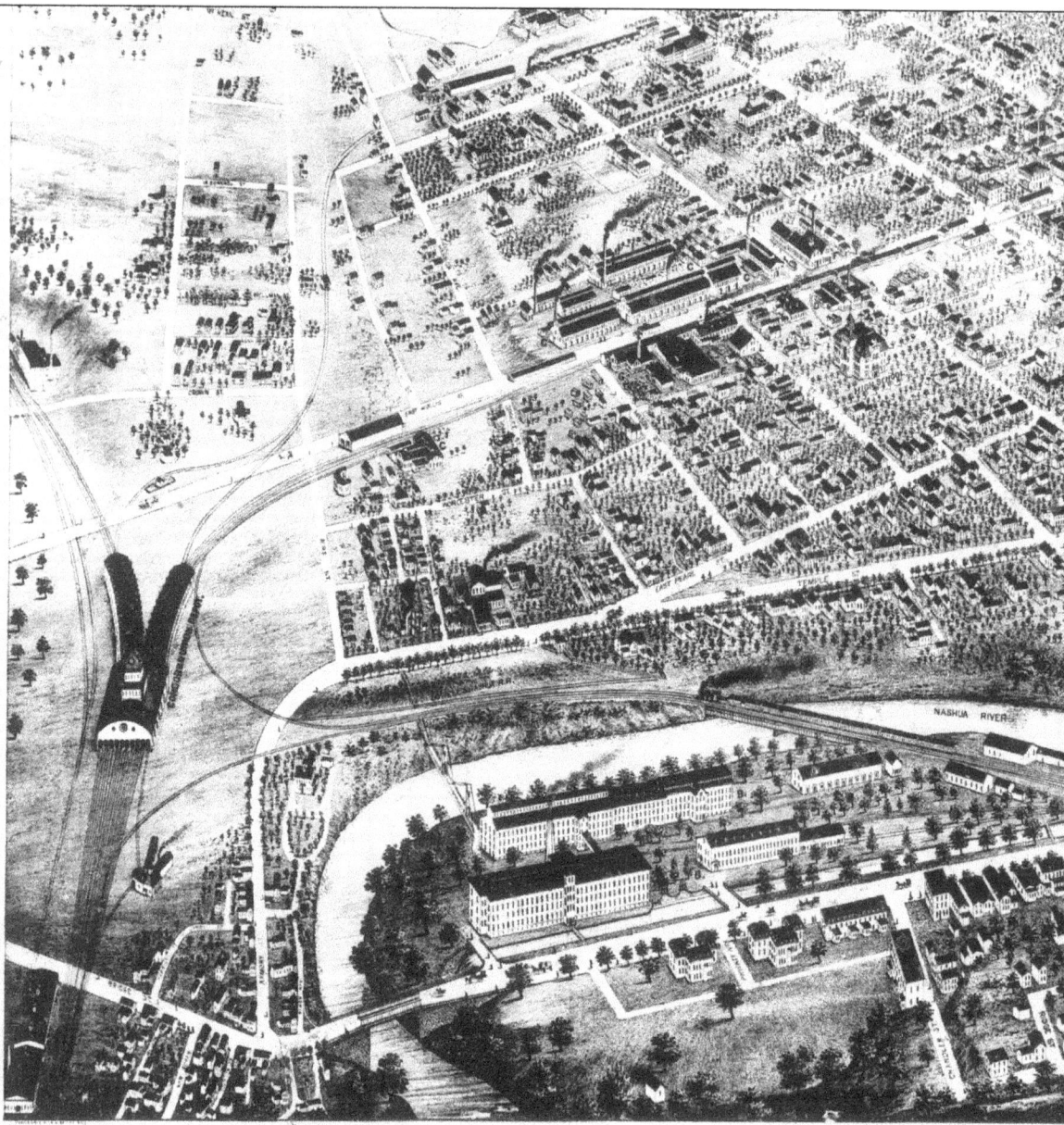

An aerial panoramic view shows old Nashua in 1875. The population count at this time was around 12,000. Banks and industry were beginning to proliferate and housing for textile workers and immigrants was beginning to be built. The city directory lists the following Nashua businesses: Nashua Literary Institute, apothecaries, auctioneers, ax manufacturer, banks, bedding manufacturer, billiard hall, bill collector, blacksmiths, bleachers, boardinghouses, box manufacturers, brass foundry, carpenters, carriage manufacturers, clairvoyants, clergymen, coffin manufacturers, corn doctor, dentists, and more. Some of the buildings listed at this time were

the bank building on Main Street (opposite city hall), Beasom's block, Dearborn block, Fisher's block, Foster's block, Franklin Hall, Goodrich block, Graves' building, Greeley's brick block, Harmony Hall (Odd Fellows), Laton's block, Masonic Hall, Merchant's Exchange, Morrill's block, Nashua City Library, Noyes' block, Nutt's building, Parkinson's building, post office, Railroad block, Shepard's block, Telegraph block, and Union block. They all helped to build our progressive city of Nashua.

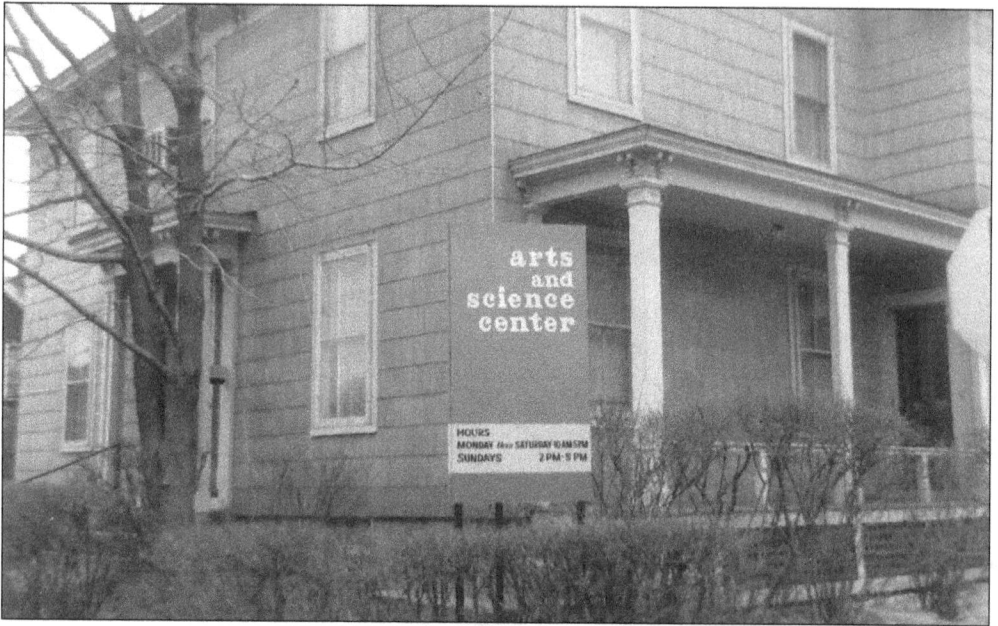

This is the Nashua Arts and Science Center on East Pearl Street in 1967 before it moved to Court Street. A brochure read, "The Center's Executive Board is working to make increased educational and cultural opportunities available to all the people of greater Nashua." The board included Margaret Swart, John Carter, Joseph Sakey, Thelma Fancy, Archie Slawsby, Robert Hamblett, Yvette Chagnon, Meri Goyette, Kenneth Mayo, and Leo Bergeron.

Upon the death of Miss Mabel Chandler in 1959, this building on the corner of Kinsley and Main Streets was bequeathed to the City of Nashua to be known as the Chandler Memorial Library and Ethnic Center. The library was formally dedicated in 1960. The barn's cupola was adorned by an antique stag weather vane, which was stolen and never recovered. It would later be replaced by an imitation.

Two

ENDEAVORS

"In the tumult and the shouting,
And the noises of the day
Keep a stillness in your spirit;
Let the quiet silence play."

In the 1850s, French-Canadian immigrants poured into Nashua to find work, many leaving their families behind. These people provided the cheap labor vital for the continued industrial expansion. Pictured here in 1918, these working girls take a break in the Lake Street Shoe Shop during World War I.

Number 112 Pine Street was owned by Max Desclos, who is pictured here with his two clerks, Larry Cote and Wilfred Brodeur. A shopper could choose from family groceries seen on shelves and sometimes hardware, kettles, tea, coffee, and other staples. The grocers were attentive and courteous and knew the patrons by name.

"In 1915 Max Desclos raised his home to put a store in. He was considered foolish for doing so. At that time the location at 112 Pine Street was remote and away from the population," narrated Louise Desclos, daughter of Tim Desclos. An old cavalry horse named "Jane" was used to deliver groceries. Later, groceries were delivered via bicycle. The grocery store became the Pine Street Market.

Local blacksmith Allan McMillian is pictured at his shop on Garden Street in 1910. Seen here, from left to right, are Frank Stafford, ? Sirois, ? McMillian, Hiram F. Rolfe, and a horse named "Dan." The children are unidentified. Leather aprons and heavy boots were needed for this type of work. Horses were the chief means of transportation for this much needed product.

The hammers swing and the anvil rings at Eddie Labrie's Lowell Street blacksmith shop. Horses needed to be shod. The horse would stand patiently as the horseshoe was nailed in place. Blacksmiths also worked iron to make axes, hatches, and other items the community needed.

39

In 1887, the Hunt Building, located at the southwest corner of Main and Factory Streets, housed the *Nashua Gazette* and *Hillsborough County Advertiser*. In recent years, this location was the site of Besse & Bryant, Nashua Co-operative Bank, and Bank Boston.

The Sargent Building on the corner of Main Street and Pearson Avenue, said to be the first brick commercial block in Nashua, was the site of Nashua's early post office. It now houses *The Telegraph* building.

The business of Herbert Rasmus McDonald, plumber, was located at No. 7 Factory Street. Mr. McDonald is seen in his derby hat en route to a service call with his helpers.

Downtown Nashua was ready for a semi-centennial parade with patriotic decorations on the Beasom and Montcalm block in 1903. Shown are the Beason, Goddard, and Montcalm Buildings. The Beasom building at the corner of Main and Factory Streets has been replaced by the Patriot Building.

This building, located at the corner of Main and Temple Streets, was home to the Nashua Telegraph Publishing Company and the Nashua Business College. The building burned down in 1922 and is the present site of the law offices of Hamblett and Kerrigan and the Granite Bank, formerly the Indian Head Bank.

Ezekiel Simon is shown with friends in the early 1900s. He appears to be a prosperous businessman. Earlier years found Nashua's population growing. Farmers from the surrounding area would come to Nashua to buy needed goods and would exchange eggs, vegetables, and poultry for merchandise by bartering. Soon after 1845, currency was the only accepted medium of exchange in larger towns.

Three city workers and horses collected hay at the Greeley farm on Concord Street. "At this time the city owned several horses which were housed on East Hollis Street at the Board of Public Works Building, also known as 'The City Barn.' The horses were also used for rubbish pick up and snow plowing," Jane and Don McAlman Sr. recall. The horses were moved from the City Barn to a location nearer to the street department. The streets were later placed under a board of public works.

Silas Breault, father of five children, part-time farmer and carpenter, and full-time millworker, lived to be 86 years old at his home on 312 Lake Street. "I remember the double-runner sled that Grandpa made for all the kids to use," Frank Mooney explains.

The start of a 1903 parade showed the Gregg wagon all set to go in front of Gage, Warner, and Whitney Company, which started business in 1857. They specialized in the manufacture of tools and machinery for the cotton industry. The Gregg's Sash and Blind Plant relocated from Goffstown to Nashua in 1870 and continued mill-working operation until the early 1960s.

Everyone knew Moss, the milkman. Daily, he delivered fresh milk in glass quart bottles to one's doorstep. In the winter, the contents would freeze and the cream rose out the top of the bottle. It is said that on the morning of October 18, 1915, Leon R. Moss was driven away by an angry crowd while trying to make a delivery at the mill gate of the Nashua Manufacturing Company. This was the beginning of the turbulent event, the 1915 strike, when 150 workers at the dye house walked off the job.

In this photograph, men move huge lead pipes for the Nashville Aqueduct, which would later become the Pennichuck Water Works in 1853. The Nashua Water Works supplied the city with water from Pennichuck Brook, a distance of about 2 miles. The Pennichuck water was forced up by pumps into a large reservoir on a hill north of the city. The Pennichuck Water Works with its series of connecting ponds has provided the city with pure water for over 150 years.

Employees were hard at work in an early sawmill at the rear of the Pennichuck Pumping Station. The hours were long and the work heavy and dangerous. Industries using wood or its by-products were essential to the economy. Attracted by excellent shipping facilities, business was booming.

The Pennichuck Water Works Utility Barn and buildings were on the north side of Front Street, facing the Nashua River and the Nashua Manufacturing Company. In 1852, the Pennichuck Water Works was started. Pipe lines and sewers were extended as running water was made available.

This photograph of a local business shows vintage hurricane lamps, streetlights, and horse-hitching posts in front of the first C.H. Avery Furniture Company on Factory Street. This store has remained in business since 1889, selling furniture to many generations of Nashuans.

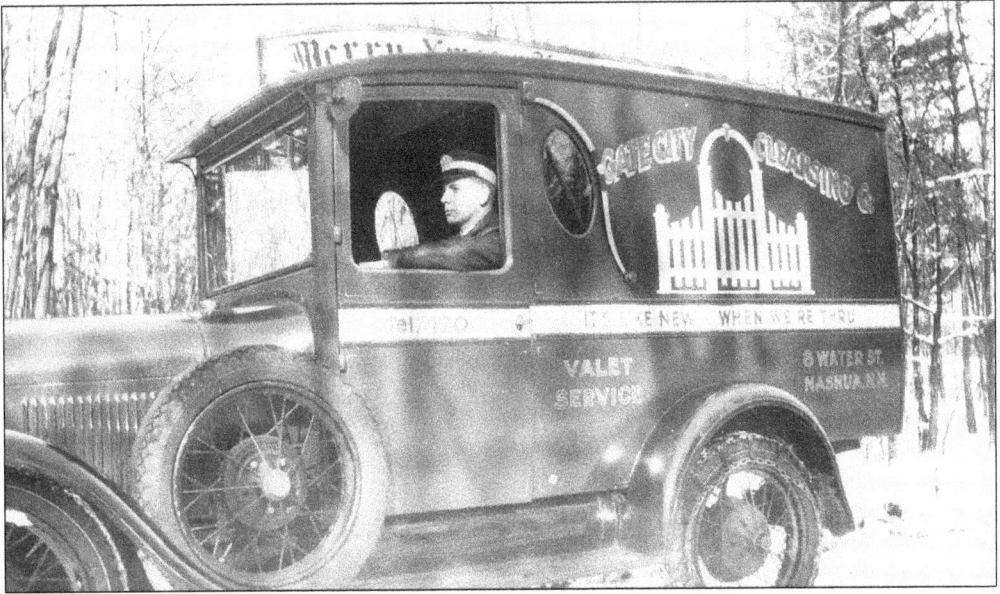

"That's my father, Rene Roy, driving for Gate City Cleaners in 1934!" Lucille Roy exclaimed. Rene was driving for Sam Dachos, who was the owner of the Gate City Cleaners. Later Rene, also known as "Doc," and his brother founded Roy's Cleaners on Canal Street, and Roy then went on to become a policeman. Policemen at that time also drove ambulances.

Automobiles and horse-power filled this Linden Street gathering in 1916 in front of the Law and Ingham warehouse.

Trade cards, a late 19th-century type of ephemeral, were a popular form of advertising. The cards were given by merchants to the general public as an inducement to purchase their goods. These cards were also advertised as a collectible as are today's baseball cards.

Fanciful advertising adorn the heading of the vendor's invoice or billing. To this day the originals are valued as collectibles. Pictures of the building, products, or the owner were common.

"From our E. Hollis Street location, we are ready to keep you warm this winter," was the slogan of the City Coal Co. Coal was used in the belly of furnaces in New England. The man of the family would go to the cellar and stoke the furnace before retiring so that the family could awaken to a warm house. The sliding of coal down the chute and into the coal bin is a sound remembered by those who also remember the hissing sound of steam coming from the radiators.

Solid rubber tires and outside hand brakes were the modern conveniences of 1916. This description fits the vehicle driven by George Gatcomb. In 1902, the first auto in the city was owned by Frank Anderson, who drove a Stanley steamer. Mr. J. Frank Stark bought the second auto, a Haynes-Apperson.

The Law and Ingham Transportation Company, Inc. was started by George E. Law in 1882 at 135 Tolles Street. Now doing business as Law Motor Freight, Inc., it is located at 27 Airport Road. The trucks shown were made in Concord in 1929 and called "Concord Trucks." Before trucks, the company made stagecoaches. This is a five-generation business with grandson Brian H. Law at the helm.

Law and Ingham Transportation Company, Inc.'s fleet of trucks made an impressive sight in the year 1925. The employees are seen beside the vehicles with the owner, Mr. Law, to one side. In 1914, Mayor William Barry was credited with the purchase of the first motor trucks used by the city's police and fire departments.

In 1920, Marcella Burnika, weaver, posed with her friend at the textile looms of the Jackson Mills on Canal Street, where the world-famous Indian Head cloth was manufactured. For hundreds of girls, the mills provided a means for earning and saving money for an education.

Bobbi Levesque showed off her finery in front of the workers' tenement housing near the mill building on Jackson Avenue. This area is now the Sanders, a Lockheed Martin Company, parking lot.

This is a photograph of Fred Boggis, who lived at 189 W. Hollis Street and who worked many years in the spinning room at Nashua Mills. Fred Boggis was the son of David Boggis, who came from England to Nashua by way of Canada.

A happy group was enjoying a respite from their work at the Nashua Corporation Metal Shop in 1941. During World War II, men and women worked together for the war effort in this shop. The Armistice Day Celebration was held in 1945.

The store front of the original Wingate Pharmacy was located at 129 Main Street, with the stairway to the Canton Chinese Restaurant located to its right. Established in 1900 by Frank Wingate, four generations of Wingate pharmacists have prevailed, culminating currently with Gary Wingate, Frank's great-grandson.

Wingate's Pharmacy has been in the downtown neighborhood since 1900. The store contained a first-class soda fountain and was noted for its effective time-tested home remedies, including the famous Marshmallow Cough Syrup and Wingate's Digestive Powder.

The Transfer Station at 166 Main Street was appropriately named. Passengers could transfer from one route to another because double trolley tracks converged in front of the store. This business was started by Christos N. Smyrnios in 1922 and continued to operate in 1934. It was next operated by George and Virginia Pialtos. In 1950, it was taken over by Peter Pleakas.

The Transfer Station not only allowed passengers to purchase streetcar tickets but also provided for the sale of newspapers, periodicals, tobacco, and high-grade confectionery items. Today it has become the Central Diner, serving breakfast and lunch in downtown Nashua.

"Let's go to Lord's Inn for New Year dinner." L. Woodbury Lord was owner of this fine eating establishment located at 12 Amherst Street from 1929 to 1936. He was known as a most hospitable host and gentleman. Later, Dr. Adrian Levesque, Dr. Wallace Buttrick, and Dr. Robert O'Neil were housed here. Across Amherst Street is the Abbot-Spalding house as well as a Greeley house and the Nashua Historical Society.

We wish you a happy and prosperous New Year

Dinner from 11:30 A.M.
to 8:30 P.M. $3.00

Little Neck Clam or Crab Flake Cocktail
Queen Olives   Boston Market Celery
Spiced Water Melon Rind
Essence of Chicken
Roast Vermont Turkey   Cranberry Sauce
Boiled Sweet Potato   Blue Hubbard Squash
Rolls
Romaine and Asparagus Salad   French Dressing
Steamed Plum Pudding   Rhum Sauce
Pumpkin or Home Made Mince Pie
Swiss Cheese   American Cheese
Sweet Cider   Coffee   Tea
Salted Mixed Nuts   Layer Raisins

Dinner $2.00
Cream of Tomato Soup
Olives   Boston Market Celery
Roast Vermont Turkey   Cranberry Sauce
Boiled Sweet Potato   Boiled Onions
Rolls
Tomato and Lettuce Salad   Russian Dressing
Steamed Plum Pudding   Rhum Sauce
or Pumpkin Pie   American Cheese
Sweet Cider   Coffee   Tea

SPECIALS

Baked Live Lobster French Fried Potatoes	$1.75
Fried Lobster Tartar Sauce	1.50
Cold Boiled Lobster	1.25
Fried Cape Scallops Tartar Sauce	1.00
Fried Jumbo Oysters Tartar Sauce	1.00

January 1, 1929

This menu was from New Year's Day in 1929. Eating at Lord's Inn was a gastronomical delight. Many lunch and dinner items that were offered on this menu are enjoyed today at the Modern Restaurant, a family-owned restaurant that has served the public for over 60 years. Its first location was at 105 West Pearl Street.

The sign read, "Manager's Week," and Thomas H. Drohan Sr. stood proudly at his store on South Main Street in 1929. The Atlantic and Pacific Tea Company was an institution throughout New England. Prices of goods shown in the window are as follows: sugar at 45¢ a pound; Old Dutch Cleanser at two for 13¢; Quaker Oats at two for 21¢. "My father and mother moved to Nashua the year of the stock market crash in 1929," son, Joseph W. Drohan, recalls.

Rochette's Diner, another fine eating establishment shown en route to its location on Main Street, is now the Fleet Bank parking lot. The diner was known for good food and good times. They were the social hub of the community. Beginning in 1872, the precursor of the diner was a horse-drawn freight wagon filled with sandwiches, boiled eggs, pies, and coffee, which served factory workers.

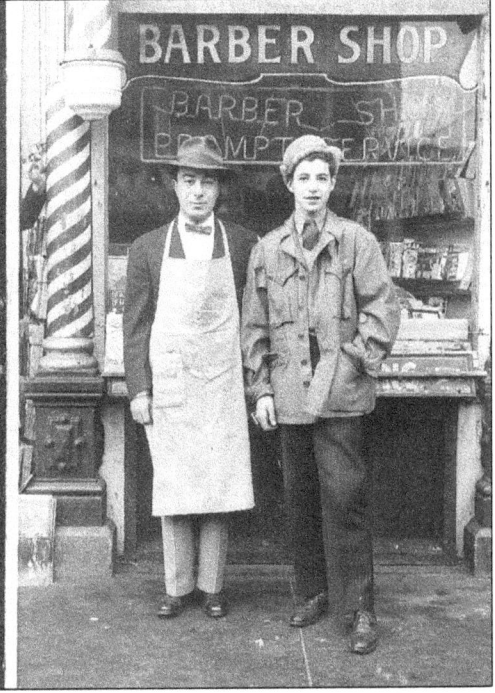

The Scontsas Store in 1935 did a little of everything. Shoes were repaired and shined, hats were blocked, hair was cut, and magazines and newspapers were sold. Pictured at the store's 175 Main Street location are, from left to right, George Scontsas, John Scontsas, and Ernest Descoteaux.

"There's no business like shoe business" at Scontsas Shoe Shine Parlor. The rhythmical sound of the polishing cloth resounded and the smell of shoe polish still lingers. Customers were greeted by name. Community events were discussed, as well as politics and local gossip. This part of the "social scene" is no longer with us.

Ravenelle Brothers grocery store at 29 McKean Street was owned by Maurice Ravenelle; his father, Luc; and his brother Ralph. There were 72 grocers in town in 1895. Shopping was a daily chore, as refrigeration did not allow food to be stored for long. Bacon was sold at 12¢ a pound, beef at 10¢ a pound, and coffee at 15¢ a pound.

An electric trolley car makes its run in front of the Transfer Station and the Spalding House. The electric car service was established in 1895 and connected Lowell and Nashua. It was the first long distance run in the country. Necessary improvements were made to the streets to meet the changes from horse-cars to trolleys. The tracks are now under layers of tar and cement, but the buildings and memories for some are still there.

This wood-burning locomotive of the Concord and Nashua Railroad was preparing to reverse direction in the roundhouse at Nashua Junction, or as it is known, the Nashua Union Station. The old roundhouse of the Boston and Maine railroad was destroyed by fire in 1909.

Referred to as the "bottleneck," Main Street needed straightening. In February 1943, the Woolworth Building burned in a spectacular fire. With reconstruction, the curve in the Montcalm Block was eliminated; the new Woolworth building was set back and erected in line with other buildings to the south.

"Coronis Cleaners had the first fur storage vault in Nashua. I remember working for Harry, Sam and 'Chappy' when I was sixteen," Alice Boggis Gabriel explains. Around the corner on the side of the Coronis building, facing where the Yankee Flyer Diner was located, the Yankee Flyer mural can now be seen. Paid for with funds donated by Nashua citizens, a bronze plaque is now in place describing the Nashua citizens seen in the painting.

A Sunday afternoon family gathering seemed to say, "Let's take a picture and then have some ice cream!" Afternoon walks after dinner were a treat joyfully anticipated by all members of the family.

The colors flew on Main Street as they passed Brockelman's Market. Parades were seen in the downtown throughout the years marking holidays. A similar parade in May 1922 celebrated the opening of the Daniel Webster Highway. A huge parade with band concerts highlighted the day.

Bicyclists joined the 1953 Centennial Day Parade in front of the 20th Century Market. The parade routes were filled with crowds in a jovial mood. Children anticipated the procession featuring various bands, military units, and civic organizations. Besides the formal parade, speeches were made by the mayor of Nashua, and were followed by sports events and fireworks.

Hammar Hardware was located at Railroad Square. The square was renamed Deschenes Oval in 1920, in honor of Private Amedee Deschenes, who died while in the service of his country in WW I. The oval has been revitalized. The granite monument listing 120 men and women who died in WW II has been cleaned, new lighting has been installed, trees and grass have been planted, and a white gazebo can be seen on the far end of the oval.

The above picture, taken in 1957, showed the second location for Carter's Men's Shop at No. 168 Main Street. At their final location, 110 Main Street, Saturday afternoon piano music and other entertainment were enjoyed by Nashuans. Downtown was the place to be in the evenings when people leisurely strolled Main Street.

64

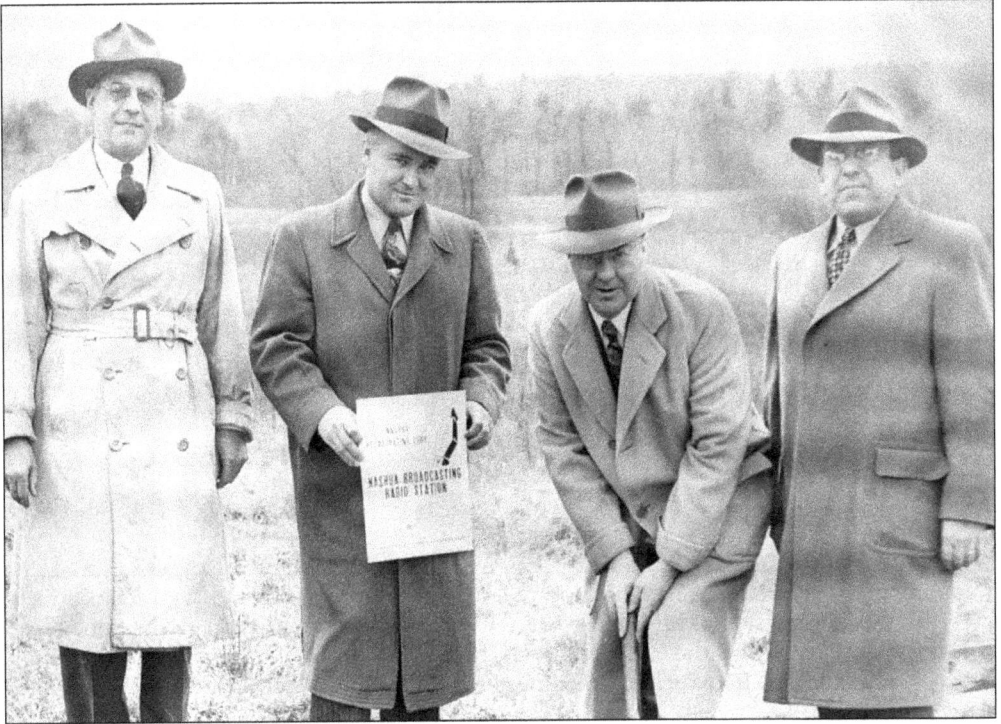

"A significant event of 1947 was the institution of the first radio station in the city," Nashua Centennial announces. Groundbreaking occurred for the home of Nashua's broadcasting radio station WOTW, located on Lund Road, on May 5, 1947. Shown from left to right are Elmer Blakey, Arthur Newcomb, Homer Wingate, and Judge Tony Guertin. Later came radio stations WSMN, WMVU, and WHOB.

The Main Street NH State Liquor Store and its employees are shown in the store's former location. The Southern NH Regional Medical Center, formerly known as the Nashua Memorial Hospital, is now located on the Main and Prospect Streets site. The Medical Center provides the latest and most sophisticated medical care to the citizens of the region.

Demolition of the Sunlight Pharmacy, located on the corner of Main and West Pearl Streets, preceded the construction of Miller's Department Store, which now houses Alec's Shoe Store. "Meet you at Miller's" was the catch-phrase of the day in the '60s, '70s, and '80s. Miller's sold everything for the lady from socks to wedding gowns to children's clothing.

Coyote Cafe's sidewalk tables are in a view of downtown Nashua. Shops, banks, restaurants, and other businesses have discovered the downtown. Lights on the trees give the street a glow, art is seen in unexpected places, and people are seen strolling once again. Destination Downtown, an organization comprised of business leaders and concerned citizens, organizes and presents activities in the downtown throughout the year, attracting people to the Nashua area.

Three

CELEBRATIONS

"Hear the flowers, feel the singing,
Taste the sunlight in your soul;"

Mr. and Mrs. John Jurago were married at St. Stanislaus Church on February 22, 1919.

Dressed in their Sunday finery in the latter 1800s, this family is ready to celebrate the Fourth of July at their home on Amherst Street. The group has gathered for a photograph to record the event. The background reveals part of their sprawling home with wood clapboard siding and shutters reflecting New England architecture at this time.

There were many activities for Nashuans both in summer and winter. Spring fishing at Jackson Falls was an activity enjoyed by many. What could be better than a day with friends with the hope of catching fish for supper? In winter, there were sleigh rides and ice-skating on Nashua's many ponds. Christmas came with the anticipation of snow, new skates, or a red sled.

Long before televised football games, Sunday afternoon meant a spirited game of croquet followed by a tall glass of iced lemonade. Croquet, a lawn game played by both sexes, consisted of knocking a rather large, wooden ball through hoops strategically placed into the ground.

These children are posed for the photographer at Saint Joseph's Orphanage, located on Main Street between Otterson and Belmont Streets. In 1901, Father Millette, of St. Louis de Gonzague Church, opened the Saint Joseph's Orphanage. In 1930, a bust honoring Monsignor Millette was dedicated and still stands in front of the church.

This view is a rare, early photograph of the exterior of St. Joseph Orphanage. During hard times, when families were left destitute because of illness or death, children were in need of the special care provided by the Catholic order of the Grey Nuns. Up to 200 children were accommodated in the facility. In the summer, outings sponsored by local businesses were eagerly anticipated by the children.

A happy group enjoyed a visit from Santa at St. Joseph Orphanage, which was decorated for the holiday. Santa would distribute candy and gifts to all. Music provided by one of the sisters at the piano accompanied the children's singing. Their voices could be heard by those walking by. Today, Santa is portrayed by Ed Lecius Jr. Each year during the Downtown Holiday Stroll, Santa is in residence at his castle at the Hunt Memorial Building on Library Hill. Here, hundreds of children visit with Santa before he departs for the North Pole.

70

Members of Jr. Goya Greek Society are dressed in authentic garb for an ethnic celebration, indicating great pride in their heritage. Until about 1902, the majority of Greeks were men who had left their relatives behind in Greece. Later, entire families began arriving. An estimated 350 people of Greek descent lived in the city by 1903.

The Lesieur family is enjoying a backyard picnic. Roland Lesieur, a well-known businessman in Nashua, is seen enjoying a quiet day with his family. The day was filled with eating good food, served by the women, and later a spirited game of baseball.

All Hallows Eve found revelers in front of the Hunt Memorial Library on Library Hill. The First Church is seen in the background. Children love to dress in costume, and this delightful group is no exception. The entrance to the children's library at the Hunt Memorial Building was located at the side door on Clinton Street. Adults used the main entrance to go to the reception desk and reading room.

A trip downtown with four children provided an outing in the life of a busy mother. Promotional pictures, such as picture-taking by a business, were common in the mid-1960s. "Our children, Robie, Robin, Meri, and Carole, were caught 'red-handed' at the 75th Anniversary of the Nashua Co-operative Bank on Main Street," C.H . Goyette, M.D. recalls. Besides delivering 10,000 babies during the course of his practice, this Nashua obstetrician delivered three of his own children, Carole, Robie, and Robin.

The Neveu family enjoyed a day at the old swimming hole at Fields Grove, which was part of Salmon Brook. Fields Grove opened in 1924 and was a popular swimming hole. "There was a bathhouse for changing clothes, one for boys and the other for girls. While in high school during the summer, Stanley Lewkowicz served as a lifeguard. He would later become a well-known doctor in Nashua," Maurice E. Chagnon, M.D. explains.

Little is known about this photograph. It shows a pyramid of barrels that was prepared for a Fourth of July celebration. Notice the American flag atop the pile.

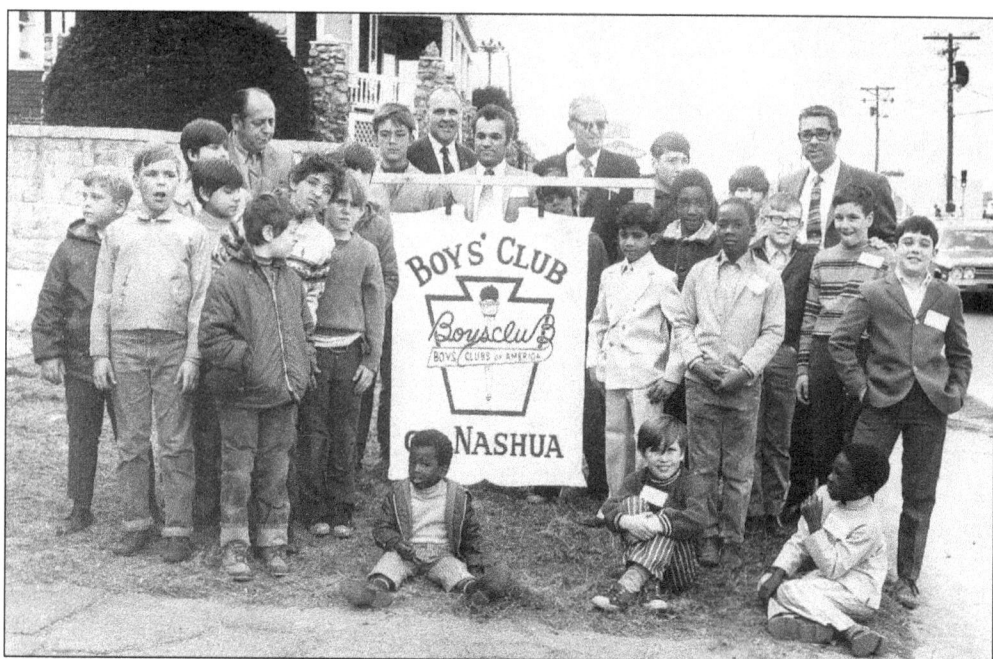

In 1971, the Boys Club was located at 315 Main Street at the old International Paper Box Machine Company across the street from what is now known as Globe Plaza. Club members and board members are seen celebrating the opening of the Boys Club in April 1971. The club provided activities and guidance for Nashua youngsters.

"Girls *do* play baseball!" The Nashua East Little League, the Radials, were sponsored by Maynard and Lesieur. Sponsorship of activities by local business was important then and now.

Members of the 1957 Church of the Annunciation YMCA Boys Basketball team pose for a photograph. The Church of the Annunciation, a Greek denomination, merged with St. Nicholas' Church to form the United Greek Community in the early 1970s.

Members of the J.F. McElwain basketball team won the title in the Nashua Industrial League by defeating the Nashua Gummed and Coated Paper Company in a three-game playoff series. The teams were sponsored by J.F. McElwain, who started shoe production on Temple Street in 1923, and by the Nashua Gummed and Coated Paper Company, commonly known as the "Card Shop."

The YMCA Basketball Team struck a pose for a photograph in 1919. In 1964, the YMCA/YWCA building on Prospect Street was completed. This building has served the needs of the community for many years. These organizations offered a variety of sports and programs to the young men and women of Nashua.

These proud faces belonged to the 1941 YMCA state volleyball champions. Did you know that the cornerstone at the YMCA Building on Temple Street was laid by the nation's chief executive, William Howard Taft? He later gave an address at the Colonial Theater in March 1912.

Nashua High Football coaches "Buzz" Harvey and Tony Marandos watched the championship game against Manchester Central. Holman Stadium was dedicated in 1937. It was used for other activities as well as football. In May 1939, more than 3,000 schoolchildren presented a May Festival in the stadium with folk dancing, singing, and sports events.

Who says "boys can't jump rope?" Jump rope, hopscotch, kick the can, and a game of marbles were played by all children. Books were read and enjoyed. A quiet pastime was called "cat's cradle" and would be played by both boys and girls. Some youngsters would be skilled with the "yo-yo." Girls were considered by some to be too delicate for strenuous play, but would play tennis and croquet and go biking and swimming.

President William Howard Taft delivered a speech at Railroad Square on March 19, 1912. He was photographed standing on the porch of the Laton Hotel when he came to Nashua to lay the cornerstone of the YMCA Building. Union (Railroad) Square is now known as Deschenes Oval.

President Harry Truman spoke at a campaign whistlestop at Nashua Union Station in 1952. Accompanying him was his daughter, Margaret. Many prominent Americans have visited in Nashua throughout the years, including Horace Greeley, when he was a presidential candidate in 1868; President Harrison in August 1889; President William Taft on March 19, 1912; and Colonel Theodore Roosevelt in 1912.

The Honorable Hugh Gregg, once mayor of Nashua and governor of New Hampshire, greeted Dwight Eisenhower and welcomed him to our city, when they were campaigning for votes.

Hubert Humphrey made an appearance at Rivier College Auditorium. He was unsuccessful in his bid for the presidency.

"Welcome to Nashua, Mr. Nixon," said Mr. Bridges in August 1971, when President Nixon visited Nashua. Many presidents visited the city, among which were Andrew Jackson in 1833, President Rutherford B. Hayes in 1877, President Harrison in August of 1889, and President Warren Harding.

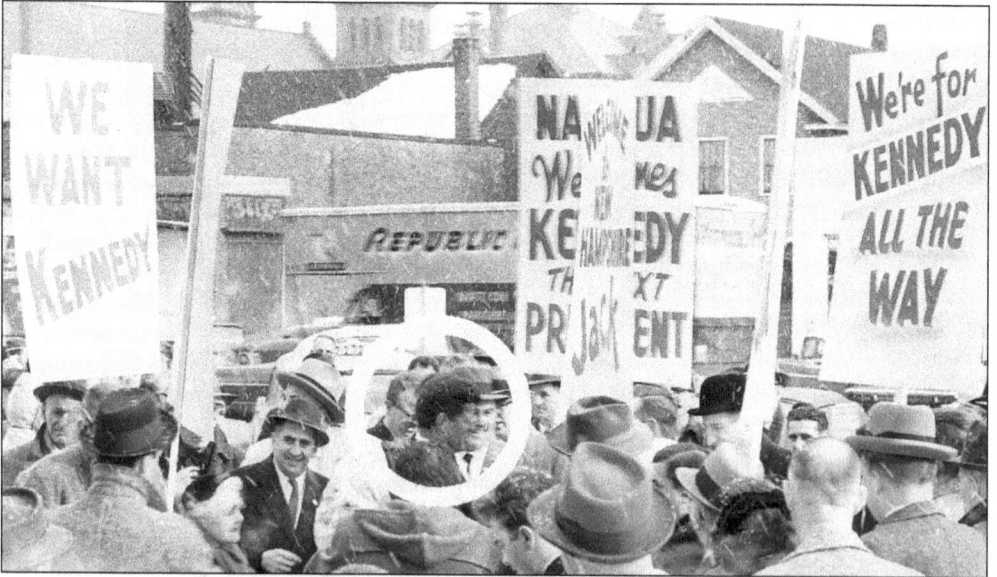

In 1960, JFK opened his campaign for the presidency in front of Nashua City Hall. "Someone asked, 'Where's the coffee?' I ran across Main Street to the Yankee Flyer Diner and then back to the press conference at City Hall with coffee for John F. Kennedy, candidate and next President of the United States of America," John Latvis remembers.

Ronald Reagan, known as the "great communicator," with his charming wife, Nancy, "worked" the crowd in 1980 during the Reagan-Bush debate at the high school gymnasium. Mr. Reagan went on to become president.

Nelson Rockefeller addressed a friendly, local crowd. Note the party symbol on the backdrop. Nashua has been the focus of national attention during the presidential primaries because New Hampshire holds the first primary in the nation.

In uniform, high school cadets posed in front of the Quincy Street School on Quincy Street in 1930. In 1887, Gen. Elbert Wheeler and Jason Tolles conducted classes in military training in

the high school. The high school cadets conducted drills, competitions, and exhibitions under the leadership of Capt. E.D. Hoitt. This building has been demolished.

The Army Navy E Award was presented to the Nashua Manufacturing Company on May 18, 1944, for producing its world-famous cotton blankets used by the military during World War II. The Jackson Mills on Canal Street also participated in the awards. The two mills were under the same management. Many employees and guests were present at this proud occasion.

As an annual event held in May, a full-dress military mass was celebrated at St. Patrick's Church on Spring Street in honor of departed heroes. St. Patrick's Church, named in honor of the patron saint of the Irish, was established in 1909 on Christmas Day. Its first pastor was the Reverend Matthew Cremer.

An Army veteran of WW II, Archie Buder was a prisoner of war for 42 months following the Bataan death march. "Archie and I were married in 1946, two years after he returned from the service," Shirley Buder stated.

Marine Staff Sgt. Allen H. Soifert was killed by sniper fire on October 14, 1983, while he was returning from a call to defuse a bomb in Lebanon. This happened nine days before the suicide truck bombing of the Marine compound that killed 253 more Marines. In 1984, a new athletic field constructed at Mines Falls Park was dedicated to his memory.

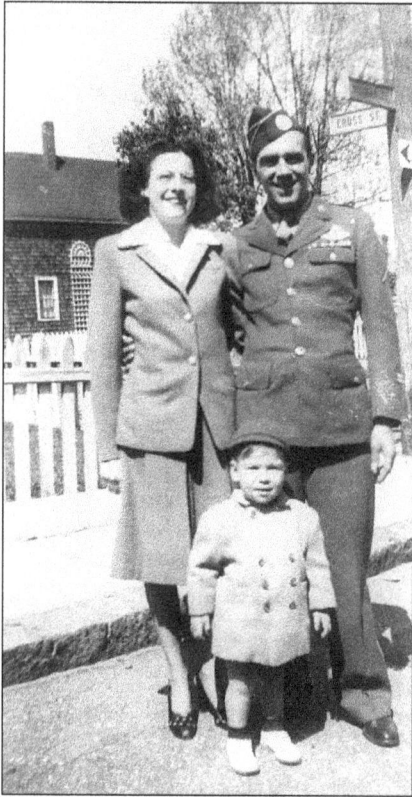

A happy homecoming showed this WW II veteran with his family standing at the corner of Lock and Cross Streets. Home never looked so good! The G.I. Bill gave many returning soldiers a chance for a college education and an opportunity to obtain low-interest loans to start businesses or buy homes.

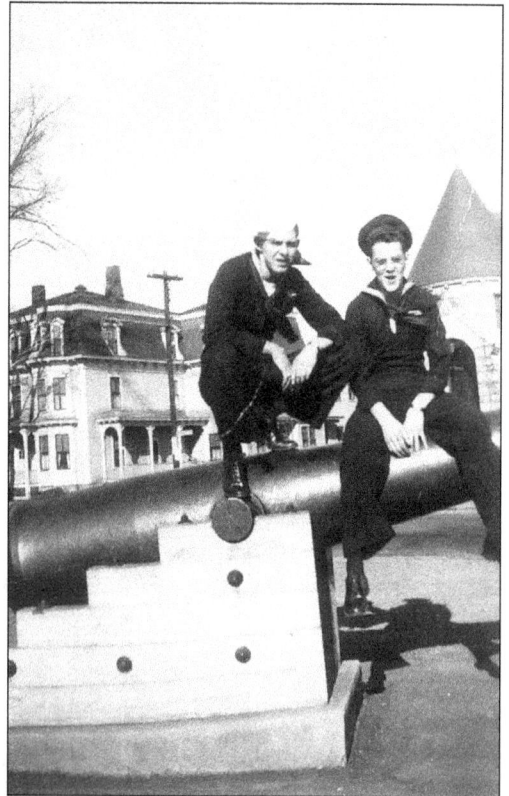

Wearing Navy uniforms, Albert Phaneuf and friend are shown sitting on the cannon at Soldier and Sailor Monument Square in 1944. The two friends served in the U.S. armed forces as did many other Nashuans. In 1940, all males between the ages of 21 and 35 were registered for the draft. Numbers were drawn at random and those accepted by the services were inducted to serve their country until the end of WW II.

Bill Ford is dressed as a Civil War veteran complete with rifle. When news was received that conflicts had broken out, a recruiting officer was appointed to aid in filling the ranks of the Third Regiment. Later, a bounty was paid to men to enlist in the Civil War. The Nashua Historical Society contains detailed Civil War memorabilia.

A Civil War veteran on horseback carried a young child down Abbot Street and into history. During the Civil War many soldiers were back home recuperating from wounds received at the battlefront. It was in 1865 that Lee surrendered. Nashuans celebrated with the rest of the North.

Civil War soldiers gathered in front of the Pilgrim Congregational Church on the crest of Temple Street, now home of One Indian Head Plaza. The Civil War erupted on April 12, 1861. Groups of men volunteered for duty in the First New Hampshire Regiment. The women of Nashua made their own contributions to the war effort by sponsoring fund-raising activities. The money received provided needed articles for the soldiers.

An elaborate horse carriage, driven by a member of the Catholic Order of the Foresters, headed for the grand parade starting at the south end of town and dispersing at Railroad Square. Among the participants were young boys driving donkey-carts down Main Street. The steam calliope made its own particular sound. Horses would follow in line. The year 1876 marked the centennial of the Declaration of Independence with a civic parade, sports, band concerts, a balloon ascension, and fireworks.

President Warren Harding is seen here on the campaign trail, before the advent of the horseless carriage. Here he participates in a parade headed south on Main Street in front of the First Congregational Church. There was always time for a parade. Boys and girls, men and women, all enjoyed the pomp and circumstance.

During the June 1903 Semi-centennial parade, the Watananach Tribe I.O.R.M. together with the daughters of Pocahontas passed Wingate's Pharmacy. Hallisey's Drug Store was located at 239 Main Street. After the parade the soda-fountain counters were filled with people sipping a sarsaparilla or indulging in an ice cream sundae.

This horse-drawn ladder wagon was on parade on the Main Street Bridge, with Nashua Manufacturing Company seen to the right, in the background. Out came the wagons and horses. Dignitaries and uniformed men marched to the bands. Women watched from the sidelines with tightened throats and tears in their eyes as the flag passed by.

These two elephants in a parade on Main Street in front of Blanchard and Currier Pharmacy, now Rice's Pharmacy, lumbered up the street. Would they remember how to find their way back to the fairgrounds? The fairgrounds was located at the site of the Fairgrounds School off Lake Street. In the evening, residents of the area could hear the roar of the lions and tigers and would hope they were tightly secured in their cages.

Parades were made for celebrations, attracting young boys and girls, and ladies and gentlemen in their finery. This scene shows spectators on the Main Street Bridge, which burned in 1924. The plans made to widen the bridge were accepted in 1927.

The music of John Philip Sousa made band music popular. Children frolicked and "the band played on" in one of the city parks in Nashua. Who can forget the band concerts in the park with blankets on the grass and children gleefully dancing to a lively tune "in the good ole summertime?"

JULY 4 1776   VICTORY   NOV. 11 1918

1861   1898

TRUGHY
CHATEAU THIERRY   ST. MIHIEL
                           ARGONNE

NASHUA, N. H. NOV. 11, 1919.

A Victory Arch on Main Street celebrated the first anniversary of the end of World War I in 1919. The arch, erected by public subscription, was dedicated to the heroes of the war. A 3.5-mile parade of eight divisions marched to the Victory Arch and then to city hall, where the soldiers were honored. The massive, white, wooden arch spanned the street and bore the inscription of "VICTORY" and the names of all of Nashua's dead heroes of World War I.

Members of the Nashua Shriners of Bektash Temple parade passed the Masonic Hall on East Pearl Street approaching Spring Street. Note the trolley tracks and cobblestone streets. The Shriners, known for their valuable contribution to children's health needs, are a highlight of our parades.

"This photograph was taken on July 4, 1925. Mother said it was the 'Horribles Parade' though she couldn't tell me why," Evelyn Lyons tells. Community participation was encouraged as neighborhoods and businesses joined in making costumes for the "Horribles." Prizes were given for the best, the worst, the funniest, and the most grotesque in various categories. A great time was had by all!

The brick Stearns Block, today the only remaining building in this photograph, is pictured behind this 1943 parade. Civic, military, and industrial groups would pass the reviewing stand. Two years later, the 1945 Armistice Day Celebration was heightened by the dedication of the World War II honor roll at Deschenes Oval.

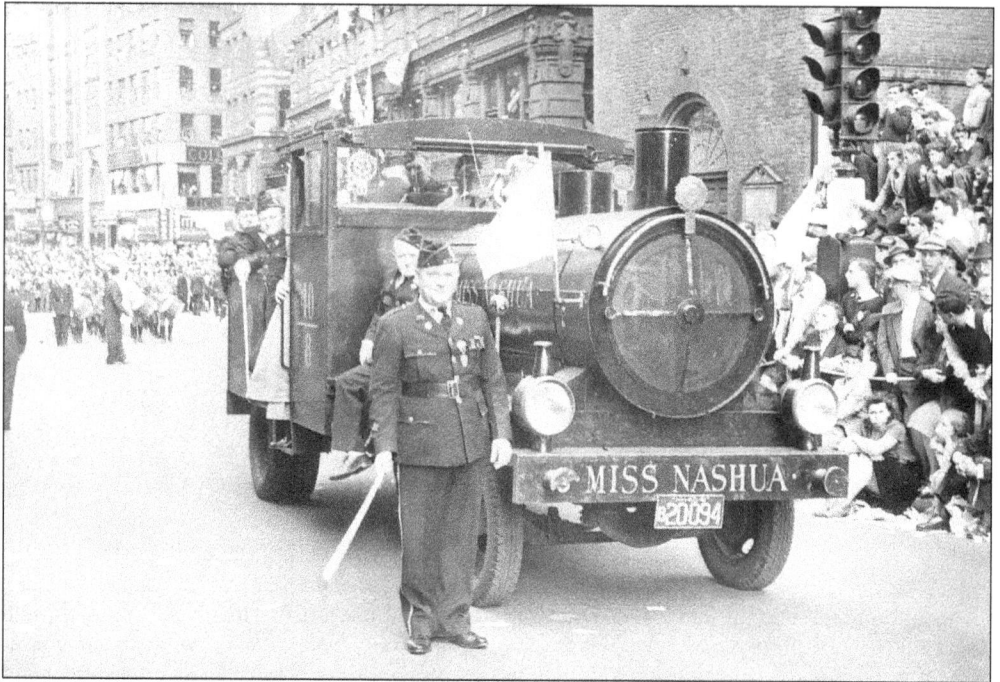

At the National Convention of the American Legion in Boston, the 40 and 8 Voiture Engine and members participated in the big parade.

A marching band passed the First National Store, now the home of Fleet Bank, in this 1953 centennial parade. This parade was part of Nashua's centennial celebration. It included a three-night performance in Holman Stadium of *Drum Beats*, a historical pageant depicting 300 years of Nashua's growth.

As a gala parade crosses the Main Street Bridge, fond memories of yesteryear come to mind. "Smell the peanuts! Hear the band! Hold your mother's hand tightly when the horses trot by and don't forget to honor your country's flag as it passes."

The YMCA float moved past a tree-shaded crowd as the 1953 Centennial parade made its way down the city streets. The parade floats were colorful, imaginative, and appreciated by onlookers. In the evening, a band concert and a fireworks display were held at Holman Stadium.

The award-winning 1948 VFW Military Band tuned up in front of Quincy Street School. Pretty, perky Katherine Winn was the majorette. Charles Coletta Sr. on the far left conducted the band.

"Not only would the diner shake, but you could lean out the kitchen door and touch the daily train as it went rolling along the tracks which were located to the right of the diner," Cynthia Kyriax Burney explains. Mary Anne Kyriax, the last owner of the Yankee Flyer Diner, recalls "Like the diners of its day, the Flyer served good, 'homemade' meals."

Four

PASSAGES

"Leaves must wither in their falling;
Butterflies must turn to dust."

This photograph shows Nashua's Bob Spence and his famous Rhythm Club, pre-WW II. Bob introduced the Rhythm Club with printed invitations to attend the "first meeting of the Rhythm Club on Saturday Evening, November 30, 1935 at eight o'clock at Mt. Pleasant School Auditorium." His business card read as follows: "Music for All Occasions." Dick Sullivan was featured at the piano. Music played an early role in the town's life; the first Regiment band was organized in 1885.

An early Nashua Symphony featured Elmer "Pop" Wilson, former music director of the Nashua School Band. Founder of the Nashua Boys' Band and the Nashua Symphony in 1929, "Pop" Wilson was also organist and choirmaster of the First Congregational Church.

In 1978, the Nashua Choral Society performed in Dulivich, England.

In 1917, a group of teachers gathered at Arlington Street School with custodian Grover Tebbets. Then, as now, both the parents' and teachers' interest in the school were vital in maintaining an efficient and progressive system. The Arlington Street School was built in 1890 under Mayor Charles Burke's administration at a cost of about $34,000.

A group of past educators posed in front of the new Spring Street High School in May 1925. In 1846, a four-room school was built on the west side of Manchester Street. In the 20th century, many public, private, and parochial schools were built, filling the educational needs of Nashua children.

In 1938 Nashua native Judge Frank B. Clancy received recognition at the dedication of the new Nashua High School on Elm Street from Mayor Alvin Lucier. This civic-minded citizen was a director of the Nashua Manufacturing Company, trustee and chairman of the Hunt Memorial Library, and member and president of the board of education for 11 years.

Dr. Frank Flagg, well-known and loved local family doctor, and his wife, Priscilla, posed in front of their home in Nashua. Dr. Flagg was one of the "old-time physicians" who made house calls. He had many interests and hobbies, one of which was painting landscapes.

Pictured are two sisters of St. Joseph's Orphanage. The sisters were selfless, kind, and pleasant. They wore black, ankle-length habits that seemed to demand respect. St. Joseph's Orphanage was on the south side of Otterson Street at the corner of Main Street. It is now the site of Nashua Ford.

The Phaneuf brothers gathered on the steps of the funeral home for the funeral of their grandfather in 1944. The facial expressions and dress of these men depict the solemn occasion. Some men came from Canada to pay their respects.

A young Al Rock was on the job as a street reporter on Main Street in Nashua. On September 13, 1947, the first radio station in the city started broadcasting. Station WOTW-AM was built on a 23-acre tract of land on Lund Road and was later joined by a sister station WOTW-FM. Arthur A. Newcomb was president and general manager of the station.

A tired cast relaxes after rehearsing for an Actorsingers' performance. As one of the first performing groups in the city, the Actorsingers helped to bring the arts to Nashua. Begun in 1956, the group still offers Nashua audiences first-class entertainment and the chance for actors and singers to perform.

Nashua's Music Man, "Pop" Wilson, conducted the high school band at many spring concerts. Nashuans enjoyed his spirited music at the school auditorium, in the open at Greeley Park, and on many other occasions. The band was a familiar part of all parades.

Well-known Nashua High School music director "Pop" Wilson dines with his new assistant, Stephen Norris. "Pop" Wilson gave many students an opportunity to learn to play an instrument and become a member of the band.

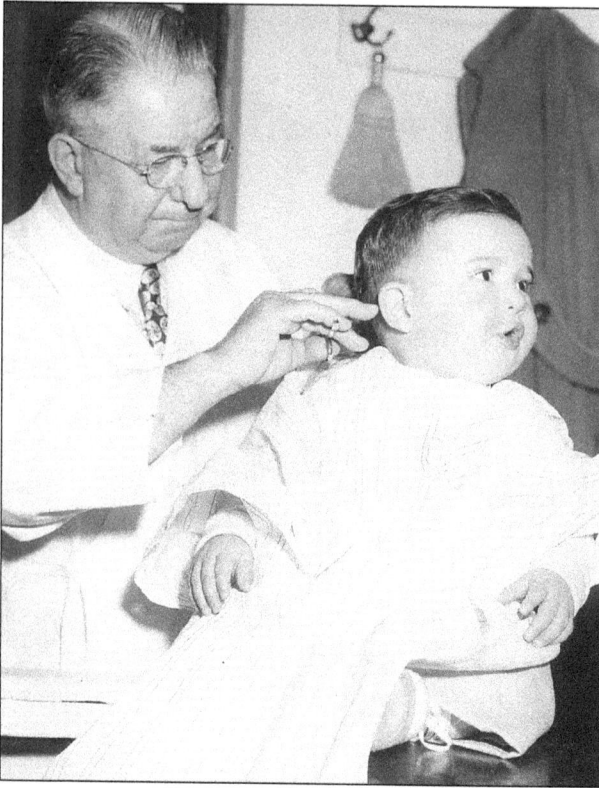

In 1955, George Annis gave ten-month-old Dean Shalhoup his first haircut. "Things have certainly changed since then," says photographer Dean Shalhoup. "Now, instead of getting a plain old haircut from a barber, I get my hair 'styled' by a young, attractive woman who uses such things as styling gel and blow dryers."

Hairstylist Isidore Guerette fashioned wigs that were in vogue at his salon, the New England Wig Center, on Main Street. He and his wife, Agnes, were known throughout the area, and participated in fashion shows. A visit to Isidore was "a must" before a party or dance! Isidore was also an avid golfer and skier.

Nashua's George "Birdie" Tebbetts, pictured on the right, managed the Cincinnati Reds during the mid-1950s. Here he meets with Gabe Paul, the team's general manager. The Brooklyn Dodgers of the National Baseball League established a farm club in Nashua in 1946. Nashua fans enjoyed watching baseball greats on the field including Don Newcombe and Roy Campanella, who played for the Nashua Dodgers.

"In January 1968 I began as Director of the Nashua Arts and Science Center. Located at 41 East Pearl Street, arts and crafts exhibitions were presented as well as art classes for children and adults. Because of the success in this small building, the Trustees were compelled to seek a larger building. The Arts and Science Center's new home was the building occupied by the Central Fire Station at 14 Court Street, now the home of the American Stage Festival," explains Jafar Shoja.

"I wanted to be in rugs from the start," F. Mahfuz stated in 1970. Sy Mahfuz explains about his father, "He was one of the finest authorities on oriental rugs. My father would often give lectures to civic organizations and church groups in the New England area. Educating people about Orientals was his passion."

"My father, Peter Scontsas, was really ahead of his time. He was never afraid of being creative and he made being in business fun. Knowing him was truly an experience," says Philip Scontsas. "Peter was 'Mr. Nashua.' I would go to him for advice on community projects. I remember Peter's enthusiastic response when I suggested year-round lights on the trees in the downtown. It took his son, Philip, to see this to fruition," Meri Goyette adds.

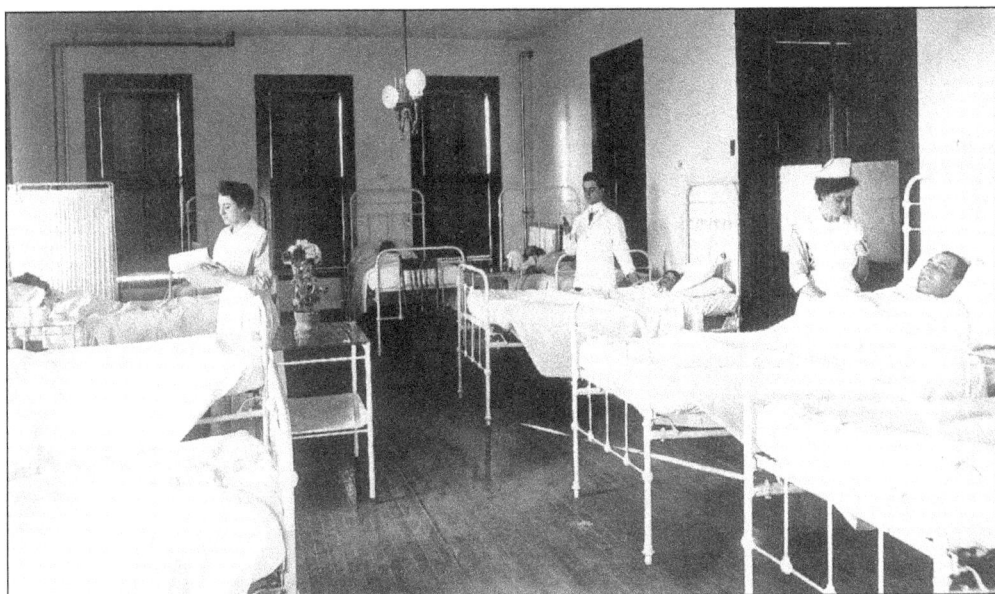

At the old St. Joseph Hospital there appeared to be only the bare necessities, but patients were treated with tender loving care. The order of the Sisters of the Grey Nuns originated in Canada and were known for their compassion toward their patients. St. Joseph's Hospital was dedicated in 1908 and is still committed to the medical needs of the community. In 1918, there was an influenza epidemic, which taxed the strength of both doctors and nurses.

The "Jeunes filles" of Nashua presented themselves in fashionable attire in 1919. For many others, life was hard with long hours of drudgery, spent mostly at work in the factories.

The elaborate furnishings and background reflected the fashionable Spence family of Nashua and the clothes of the day. Samuel Spence came to Nashua in 1894 and operated a successful department store in the Noyes Building on Main Street.

"Elizabeth Brown (1896–1958) was the granddaughter of J.C. Wheeler, who moved from Littleton in 1830 to marry a local girl. As a 'rite of passage' in the early 1900s, a young lady put her hair up at age 16. This picture from 1912 commemorates that event. Now, seven generations later, still living in the Nashua area are her daughter, Marvis Mellen; granddaughter, great-granddaughters and one great, great, granddaughter born in 1998," Frank H. Mellen narrates.

A touch of the Old Country in America is evident in this picture of Grandpa Moss, Priscilla Flagg's grandfather. The year was 1920. As a child, Priscilla would occasionally accompany Grandpa on his rounds and they would stop along the way for ice cream—precious memories from times past.

"Dad is shown in front of his tomato plants pretending to hoe the beans in July, 1945," wrote Dexter Arnold, Frank's son. Farming in Nashua was found at many locations. Families worked side by side for the harvest, bringing excess produce to the marketplace.

The year was 1914. The family of Ezekiel Simon is pictured with their daughter, Eva, mother of Nashua attorney S. Robert Winer. The family resided on Cottage Avenue where this photograph was taken.

The Juraga family, Amelia, John, and Bernice, "sat" for a formal portrait. Portraits of individuals and family groups were cherished and displayed in the parlor. This picture was probably taken by the Nashua Photo Company at its studio at 103 Main Street. Here special times of Nashuans were recorded. Another Nashua photographer, Frank Ingalls, took pictures of buildings and the environment, from around 1872 into the 1890s. He was seen climbing towers and chimneys to capture views.

Two unidentified tots are photographed riding off on a "trike" after buying penny candy at the neighborhood store. This was the simple life when a trip to the store for candy was a treat! Today, a stop at Martha's Sweet Shoppe on Main Street is still a treat. Martha's is the candy store to visit, especially at Eastertime when chocolate bunnies and Easter eggs of all sizes are displayed; Ethel Fokas hostesses the display.

"After passing through Ellis Island from Greece in 1946, we found that America was heaven for us! Arriving in Nashua on a Tuesday, I got a job in a shoe factory on Wednesday at $35 a week," recounts George Tsiaras. During the early years of the 20th century many Greeks, as well as Polish, Lithuanian, and Jewish immigrants, came to settle in Nashua. Adjustments to their new world were taken in stride and they soon became an integral part of the community.

These smiling faces from 1938 belonged to the students of the Country Club School, a one-room school on Lowell Road, now South Main Street. The teacher was Miss Barbara Mulvanity. One student in the photograph is Alice Barsanti Nolan; three others are from the Boggis family, including Alice, grade three, Donald, grade two, and Marion, grade one.

These kindergarten children eventually became the high school graduating class of 1939, 80 years after the first high school graduation in the city was held in 1859. A few of the children in this photograph were Marion Williams Britton, Victoria Kopka, and Robert O'Neil, who later became a respected practicing urologist in Nashua for many years.

This is a class picture of students at the Arlington Street School. One of the students, Samuel A.T. Spence, is pictured in the second row, third from right. At this time, hats were an essential part of the wardrobe, as can be seen by the children's attire. This fashion accessory was provided to the community by milliners, who would make them by hand.

Marian Herbert Chandler was one of the students dressed for this graduation day at Spring Street High School. The Spring Street High School was built in 1875 and used as a high school until 1905, at which time it became a grammar school. As noted from the Nashua Centennial Book, "In 1872 Spring Street burying ground prepared for new High School building. Bodies were removed to Hollis Street cemetery."

The Girls Sewing Circle, including Noemie Duchesneau Dambroise, gathered for a group photograph in 1918. The Sewing Circle was a women's social "get-together," where sewing was done at the home of one of the ladies and where, in the course of the afternoon, over afternoon tea, news of the community was exchanged.

Family and friends relaxed at the Tolles farm on Main Dunstable Road near Tolles Pond. Rich soil encouraged farming in this area, and many Nashua families tilled the soil, producing fruits and vegetables both for their own use and for the marketplace. Produce was often used as barter in exchange for needed services, supplies, or equipment.

Sunday afternoon activities at the Schoonmaker home included games, music, and visiting with friends and family. The parlor organ and piano were as popular then as television is today. Someone would start to play a familiar tune and soon all would gather around to sing, leaving their cares behind.

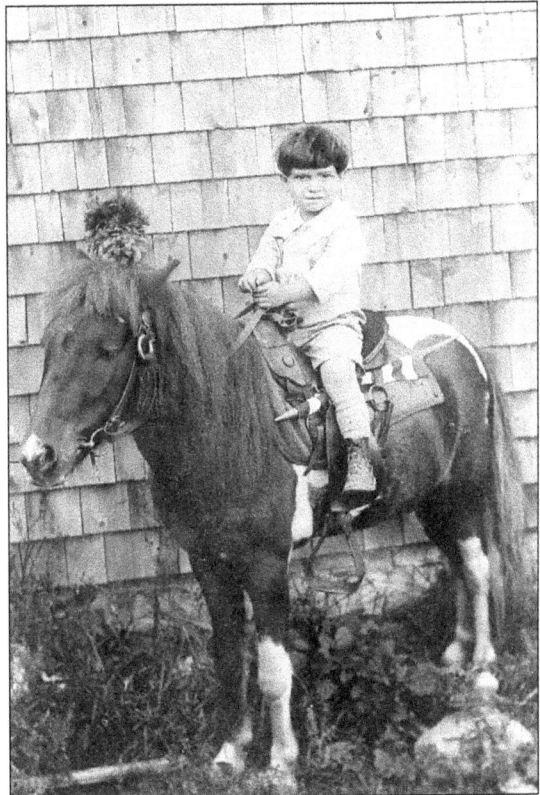

H. Robert Weisman is shown on his "first set of wheels" in 1925. Bob Weisman lived off Canal Street with his family. This photograph was taken by a roaming photographer, who arrived with horse and camera. Being the youngest of the family, Bob was chosen by his mother for the photograph. This little boy grew up, went off to college, and founded Weisman, Tessier and Lambert, an insurance and financial advisory group.

"The Tolles Street Gang" starred Bernard Pastor. Pictured in their knickers, in front of 112 Tolles Street are, from left to right, 'Tootsie' Coutsonikis, 'Bernie' Pastor, Robert Donah, Ray Baker, Ray Barriault, Irving Pastor, 'Bootsie' Donah, and Paul Boire. Bernie Pastor became the owner of Fletcher's Appliance. Boire Field is named after Paul Boire, who was the first Nashua pilot to give his life in WW II.

" 'The Madigan Irish Trio,' Robert, John, and Francis sit on their doorstep at 30 King Street on Crown Hill waiting to play football at Marshall Field. The strains of 'When Irish Eyes Are Smiling' could be heard coming from the kitchen on any given day, sung by grandfather Francis Madigan, a native of Limerick, Ireland," Patty Ledoux, daughter of Jim Madigan, recalls.

Muriel Neveu Francoeur and her mother watched for the train to take her to boarding school. Muriel is seen sitting on her suitcases "waiting for the train to come in." The Union Station, once busy with incoming and outgoing trains, was torn down in 1965. Built in 1860, it was a Nashua landmark. Many regret the razing of the Union Station, which holds both sweet and sorrowful memories.

A young woman was dressed fashionably for a Sunday outing. Nashua stores offered millinery, dresses, and gloves, which were a necessity in every woman's wardrobe. Mothers and grandmothers were often put into service sewing dresses for the girls in the family. It is interesting to note that the city directory for 1872, many years before this photograph was taken, lists 99 dressmakers and 21 milliners.

Uniforms and bobbed hair were in vogue at St. Joseph Orphanage in Nashua during the 1930s. St. Joseph's Orphanage served homeless children of the area from the year 1900 until 1963. It was located between Otterson and Belmont Streets. Included in this photograph is Rita Briere.

The Ladies of Charity sewed for the St. Joseph Orphanage & Hospital. These women and others spent many hours doing volunteer work for the needy while enjoying the company of each other. Meeting regularly in the afternoon, ladies would sew blankets and needed clothing for the children. Nashua's first ladies' volunteer group, the Good Cheer Society, was founded in 1885 to make home visits to people who were ill and house-bound. It expanded into a visiting nurse service and is still active as Home Health and Hospice Care.

People dressed in muffs, toques, and knickers gathered around this early Indian Motorcycle with sidecar. This photograph taken on Mulberry Street, which seems to have been staged, shows a woman in the driver's seat! At this time, in 1901, Milton A. Taylor was mayor of Nashua. His term in office saw a new mode of transportation arrive, "the horseless carriage."

In the early years of the 20th century, many Greek families came to settle here and raise families. This photograph shows the traditional roasted lamb on a spit at Easter in 1966. Reunions and celebrations were frequent events in the social structure of newcomers to Nashua. Food, music, high spirits, and laughter are memories to be cherished.

Stanley Nadolski worked in the bleachery at the Nashua Mills in the 1930s. The Poles, Irish, French-Canadian, and other immigrants were hired to work in the Nashua Mills, which were built along the river, where long hours and low wages were normal.

In this photograph, men of the Polish community are pictured leaving the Nashua Manufacturing Company Bleachery after a 12-hour workday. Pictured are Stanley Nadolski and John Juraga. Daniel Abbot, called "the Father of Nashua," started the Nashua Manufacturing Company. The property, a large tract of land of several hundred acres in size, was later developed. Streets were laid out, buildings were erected, and plans were made for a growing township.

A log cabin can be seen in Greeley Park in this 1944 scene. This park has 125 acres of land with spacious lawns used for picnics and relaxation. The hurricane in 1938 felled many trees in the park; however, many trees remain. This property was purchased by Joseph Greeley in 1801 and passed on to his son, Joseph Jr., and Joseph Jr.'s son later willed it to the City. A gift of $5,000 by Joseph Cotton, with the City matching the amount, made possible the development of Greeley Park. It is the hub of the City's park and recreational system.

Walter Markewich worked hard haying on a farm on Pine Hill Road in 1947. Farms were on the edge of town, and a walk to the downtown was enjoyed by family members. In earlier days, prosperous farms were found in outlying areas of the city. The farm of Zachariach Shattuck of Round Road off Amherst Street was one such farm. Shattuck's land was comprised of 400 acres.

Lester Gidge is seen here with his mother. This little boy would grow up to be a prolific inventor. Among his many accomplishments, Mr. Gidge developed components for the Hubble space telescope, guidance systems for space exploration, machines for picking cranberries and blueberries, and a self-watering flower pot.

Well-known Nashuan and inventor Lester Gidge is shown sliding in the park. "This photograph was taken at our Nashua Industrial Machine Shop yearly picnic at Pulaski Park. The children are those of shop employees," Lester Gidge recalls. Nashua was the home of other inventors, such as Elias Howe, of sewing machine fame; George Rollins, the inventor of a breech loading cannon; and Henry A. Sevigne, who invented the bread-wrapping machine in March 1911.

Mailman Ray Ouellette helped three-year-old Jennifer Lambert mail her letter to Santa. This charming photograph is credited to Michael Shalhoup, a former photographer, sports editor, and retired managing editor of *The Telegraph*. Joining *The Telegraph* in 1952, he earned numerous awards for his work. (Courtesy of *The Telegraph*, photographed by Mike Shalhoup.)

Fields Grove, a municipal swimming pool, beach, and play area, was the summer spot for Nashuans during the 1960s. This park, named for a landholder who allowed access to it through his property, provided hot weather enjoyment for thousands. Located on Salmon Brook, it was the scene not only of daily picnics but of evening courting. After a day's work, a cool dip in the water was a treat. Pollution of the Salmon Brook forced the City to close the area.

Posing in her fashionable 1920s attire is Madeline Lawrence Caron of Nashua. Madeline and her husband had six children who lived in Nashua: Delphis, Elaine, Estelle, Gloria, Raymond, and Rena. Nashua ladies were seen as fashion minded. People of this era also placed strong emphasis on family ties and religion.

These three men lived to see their many projects taken to completion. Frank Harvey (banker), Sam Tamposi (real estate developer), and Robert Cross (banker) showed that people come together to work for the community. These citizens were instrumental in the growth and development of Nashua.

This 1952 American Legion baseball team was coached by the Cleveland Browns' John Kissell, shown on the far left. Also pictured are coaches John Shubelka and Paul Moriarty. The Nashua Pirates was Nashua's franchise baseball team. They stayed in the city through 1987. Today we have the "Nashua Pride," whose players aspire to the big leagues. Baseball is still played at Holman Stadium. Under the administration of Mayor Donald C. Davidson, the old field has been newly reconstructed providing a first-class stadium for baseball fans.

This 1963 American Legion baseball team is shown in street attire at a presentation at city hall. Greg Landy is pictured in the second row, fourth from left. When the team played the inmates at the state prison, the future Detroit Lions quarterback hit a ball that dropped into the prison's 100-foot-tall chimney!

In the 1950s children frolicked at the North Common fountain on Sargent Avenue. From *the Nashua experience*: "No separate department to maintain parks and recreation areas was really needed during most of the nineteenth century, because there were only two such areas, North Common and South Common, where the main task seems to have been cutting the hay in the summer; planting shade trees and keeping up walkways do not require large sums of money. In 1896 three Park Commissioners were designated, marking the birth of the Park and Recreation Department as we know it today." It was Mayor Sargent who secured the North Common, a 40-acre area and site of the Amherst Street School. Sargent, chosen mayor of Nashua in March 1871, was seen as an energetic and progressive man. Between 1946 and 1949, Mayor Oswald Maynard developed this project as a park.

"Should you hurry toward tomorrow
Every magic day must die.
Now is all the time for loving:
Getting all, by letting go."

—David D. "Doc" Cote

www.ingramcontent.com/pod-product-compliance
Lightning Source LLC
Chambersburg PA
CBHW050924150426
42812CB00051B/2141